Dad Gets a Job

by Peggy Bresnick Kendler

illustrated by Robbie Shont

Scott Foresman
is an imprint of

PEARSON

Glenview, Illinois • Boston, Massachusetts • Mesa, Arizona
Shoreview, Minnesota • Upper Saddle River, New Jersey

Illustrations by Robbie Shont

ISBN 13: 978-0-328-39434-0
ISBN 10:   0-328-39434-3

Annie Borden sat on the front porch. She was talking with her best friend, Sue. Sue's family was moving out of town. "I'll miss you," Sue said sadly.

"I'll miss you more," Annie said. She was afraid that her own family might have to move too. But she didn't tell Sue.

Annie gave Sue one last hug. She watched Sue walk home. She felt so sad.

Annie went inside her home. The house used to be toasty warm. Now it was cold. Annie wished she had some more sweaters to wear.

Life was not always like this. Two years ago, Annie had lots of clothes to wear. Her father still had his job. He worked as a bookkeeper. He brought money home every week. The family always had food. Annie and her older brother Tom had toys too.

Annie remembered when everything changed. A year ago, in 1929, the stock market crashed. Annie's dad had told her about stocks. He said, "You could give money to a company to help run it. Then you owned a small part of that company. If the company made money, you made money too. If it didn't, then you didn't. But then suddenly, stocks were worth nothing. Banks were out of money. Rich people became poor people. Companies went out of business, and people lost their jobs." They called this time the Great Depression.

Sue was not the only one who had
to move away. Her brother Tom's friend,
Hank, moved to California to live with his
aunt.

Tom had a job cleaning a neighbor's
barn. He made a dollar a day. Annie tried
to sell eggs by the road. But no one would
buy them. Annie's father kept looking for
work.

Annie's mother looked sadly out the window. "This is the first year I won't plant tulips. There's no money to buy bulbs," Annie's mother said.

Annie felt very sad. She knew how much her mother loved the beauty of the flowers.

Just then, Annie's father came home. "Dad!" Annie called out. Annie's father used to have a great sense of humor. Now he hardly ever smiled.

"Any luck?" asked Annie's mother.

Annie's father shook his head. Every day, he looked for work. He waited outside buildings where people might give out jobs. There was always a crowd of men.

Annie's family sat down to dinner. "At least we have corn and potatoes from our farm," Annie's mother said. "We have fresh milk from our cows. What we can't sell, we can keep for us. We're lucky we live on a farm."

Just then, there was a knock on the door.

Annie ran to open the door. She recognized their friend, Mr. Rice. Mr. Rice didn't live on a farm. Annie's mother knew he was hungry. She often invited him and his family to dinner. "My wife knit this blanket," he said, kneading it with his hands. Annie's mother took the blanket. She handed Mr. Rice two bottles of milk. "Will you stay for dinner?" she asked. "Another time, Mrs. Borden," he said. "Thanks."

The next morning, Annie's father left early. "I'll get bread today," he said. Annie knew that the bread lines were very long. Often more than a hundred people would stand in line to get free food. It could take hours before her father got home!

Annie and Tom were about to doze off, when their father came home. He was smiling!

"I have a new job!" said Annie's father happily. "I am the new mechanic down at Hillson's Garage!"

Annie's mother looked at her husband. "A mechanic? Can you do that?" she asked.

"I fix our car. I know how engines work," he said. "To feed my family, I can do anything."

"Gifts for everyone!" said Annie's father. He handed the children new pencils. Then, he pulled out a small bag. "By spring, these should be blooming," he said.

Annie's mother opened the bag. Inside were tulip bulbs!

Everyone talked and joked as they ate dinner. It was the happiest day!

Annie's father left for work early the next morning. This time, he was whistling. He would bring home 15 dollars every week. That was enough money to keep the family going. It was also enough money for both Annie and Tom to get new clothes.

On the first nice day, Annie and her mother went out to plant the tulip bulbs. They dug small holes for the bulbs in the corner of the garden. "I'm so glad Dad found a job," said Annie.

Annie's mother smiled at her. "So am I," she said. "After spring showers, these bulbs will be sprouting and growing into tulips. Then we'll remember how lucky we are."

The Great Depression

In October 1929, the stock market crashed. Many banks went out of business. People lost all the money they had saved in those banks. Rich people suddenly became poor. The following years were known as the Great Depression.

The Great Depression was a very tough time for people in the United States. Many people couldn't find any work. Some families lost their homes. They had to move away. Children stopped going to school. They did not have shoes or clothing to wear.

Many people in the United States were very poor at that time. Many shared what they could with others.

The Great Depression did not end until 1939.